THE MAGIC OF
RED

The Color Books are dedicated to the Rainbow Child in all of you

Series concept by Ayman Sawaf
Copyright © 1995 by Enchanté Publishing
MRS. MURGATROYD Character copyright © 1993 by Enchanté
MRS. MURGATROYD™ is a trademark of Enchanté

Written by Neysa Griffith.
Character created by Steven Duarte.
Illustrated by Deborah Morse.
Edited by Gudrun Höy and Anne Sheldon.

Enchanté Publishing
P.O. Box 620471
Woodside, CA 94062

Printed in Singapore

Library of Congress Cataloging-in-Publication Data
Griffith, Neysa
The magic of red / written by Neysa Griffith; character created by Steven Duarte;
illustrated by Deborah Morse. - lst ed.
     p.   cm.
Summary: Playful verses and illustrations invite children to enter the magical
world of colors.
ISBN 1-56844-025-1 : $6.95
1. Red —Juvenile poetry. 2. Colors—Juvenile poetry.
3. Children's poetry. American [1. Red —Poetry. 2. American poetry.]
I. Neysa Griffith.   II. Morse, Deborah, ill.   III. Title.
PS3557.R4893M32   1994
811' .54—dc20   93-34813

First Edition
10 9 8 7 6 5 4 3 2 1

THE MAGIC OF
RED

Written by Neysa Griffith
Illustrated by Deborah Morse

énchanté Publishing

Red is the color of cherry delight,
    sweet candy apples—take a big bite.
Red is the nose of a clown at the fair.
Red's a balloon flying high through the air.

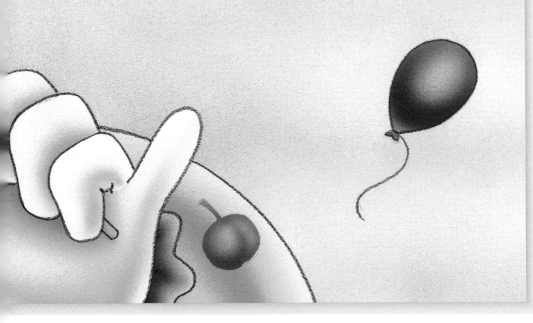

Red is the badge of the brave and courageous.
Acting like red is acting outrageous.

Red is a rocket that flies at great speed.
Red is a child who will take the lead.

Red will protect you in the dark of the night;
a fearless friend that will make things all right.
Red is the anger we sometimes show.
Red can help out when we must say "no."

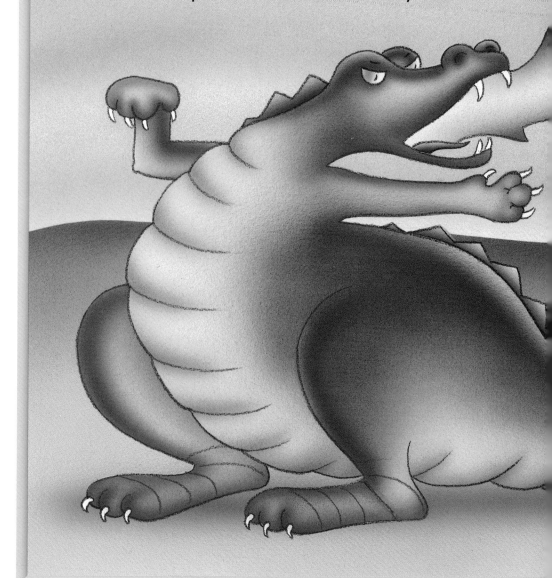

Red's a volcano erupting with fury,
a fire truck racing to help in a hurry.

Red stop signs tell you when not to go.
You're safe and secure, with rules that you know.

Red for the robin, red for the fox.
Keep your feet warm in little red socks.

Gnomes mine red rubies deep in the earth,
splendorous gems of immeasurable worth.

Tomatoes which ripen turn red on the vine;
yummy strawberries, so sweet and so fine.
A little red wagon to carry your goods
to a red schoolhouse that's close to the woods.

Red is impulsive, it's hurried and fast.
Red is the color without future or past.

Red knows only now and no other way.
Red isn't tomorrow, it's only today.

Red is the rhythm of a beating drum.
The spirit of red is adventuresome.

Red is the spark of your inner fire.
Red is achieving your deepest desire.

Red is the color to make a new start.
Red is the rose that blooms in your heart.

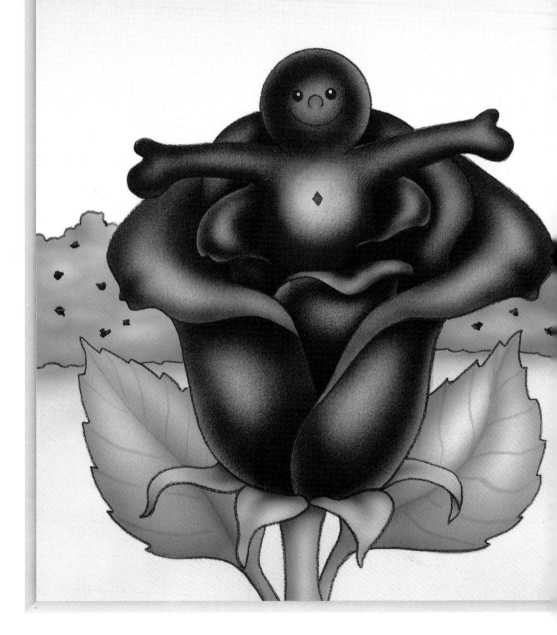

Write a love message in letters of red.
Say anything that pops into your head.

The magic of red is inside of you.
It can happily help you in all that you do.
To make red your friend,
close your eyes and pretend...

You are standing tall on a mountain crest,
feeling fantastic, feeling your best.
Imagine the tail of a comet aflame,
sailing through space, spelling out your own name.

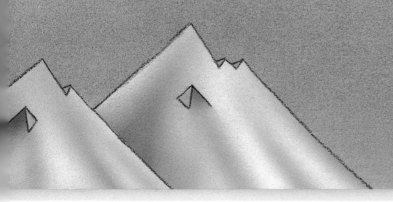

Red starbursts of fireworks set the night sky aglow.
Now are you ready? Then get set and go!

Enchanté books are dedicated to enhancing the general well-being of children by encouraging them to use their own imagination and creativity to explore their thoughts and feelings. Each story is a symbolic journey into the magical world of self, where children discover the power they have within. Enchanté offers high quality hardcover picture books with accompanying activity books and parents' guides which include:

And Peter Said Goodbye
Exploring Grief
Exploring Grief With Your Child

Painting the Fire
Exploring Anger
Exploring Anger With Your Child

Red Poppies for a Little Bird
Exploring Guilt
Exploring Guilt With Your Child

The Rainbow Fields
Exploring Loneliness
Exploring Loneliness With Your Child

Nightmares in the Mist
Exploring Fear
Exploring Fear With Your Child

William's Gift
Exploring Hurt
Exploring Hurt With Your Child

Knight-time for Brigitte

For more information call:
1-800-473-2363

or (415) 529-2100
fax # (415) 851-2229

enchanté Publishing